A Valentine's Day DRAWING Treat!

CAPSTONE PRESS
a capstone imprint

by Jennifer M. Besel

illustrated by Lucy Makuc

First Facts are published by Capstone Press,
1710 Roe Crest Drive, North Mankato, Minnesota 56003
www.capstonepub.com

Library of Congress Cataloging-in-Publication Data
Besel, Jennifer M.
  A Valentine's Day drawing treat! / by Jennifer M. Besel.
     pages cm. —(First facts. Holiday sketchbook)
  Includes bibliographical references and index.
  Summary: "Step-by-step instructions and sketches show how to draw common Valentine's Day images
and symbols"—Provided by publisher.
  ISBN 978-1-4765-3094-9 (library binding)
  ISBN 978-1-4765-3425-1 (ebook pdf)
  ISBN 978-1-4765-3449-7 (pbk.)
  ISBN 978-1-9771-8898-4 (pbk.)
1. Valentine's Day in art. 2. Drawing—Technique—Juvenile literature. I. Title.
  NC825.V34B47 2014
  743'.893942618—dc23   2013005603

Editorial Credits
Juliette Peters, designer; Kathy McColley, production specialist

Photo Credits
Capstone Studio: Karon Dubke, design elements, 5 (photos); Shutterstock: Kalenik Hanna

Printed and bound in China. 3742

Table of Contents

Heart Art

Love letters and roses
  and good treats to chew.
Valentine's Day is fun,
  and learning to draw is too!

Wouldn't you love to draw Valentine's Day pictures? Then this book is for you. Just follow these tips and the simple steps on each page. You'll be drawing heartfelt pictures in no time.

TIP ① **Draw lightly.** You will need to erase some lines as you go, so draw them light.

TIP ② **Add details.** Little details, such as hearts or silly signs, make your drawings extra thoughtful.

TIP ③ **Color your drawings.** Color can make a lovely drawing even better!

You won't need a bow and arrow to make people love your drawings. But you will need some supplies.

drawing paper

eraser

pencil

colored pencils or markers

pencil sharpener

Sharpen your pencils, and get ready to draw all the sights of Valentine's Day. **It will be a treat!**

Heart Full of Love

Stories say Cupid's arrow fills a heart with love. But an arrow's not the only thing that spreads love. Your drawing can do that too.

Final

Don't Forget!
Erase lines that go under something or lines that aren't needed anymore. For example, erase the parts of the circles inside the heart in step 2.

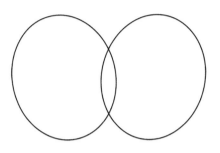

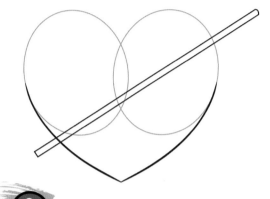

1
Draw two circles of the same size overlapping each other.

2
Draw curved lines coming from the outsides of the circles. They should form a point. Draw a long, thin rectangle through the heart.

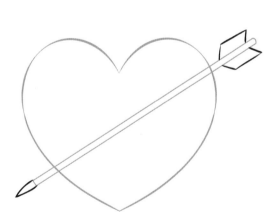

3
Draw a point on one end of the rectangle. Draw two slanted rectangles on the other end.

4
Draw a triangle around the pointed end of the arrow. Add detail lines to the small rectangles on the other end.

Floating on Air

Celebrate the day with this project. Draw some "I Love You" balloons, and pop someone's bad day.

Final

1 Draw three ovals slightly overlapping one another. Add one curved line inside each oval.

2 Write "I" on the line inside the first oval. Write "love" inside the second and "you" inside the third. Add a small rectangle then a triangle under each balloon.

3 Add detail lines and circles to the balloons. Draw two small ovals near the triangle under each balloon. Below the balloons, draw a bow with three tails. Finally, draw thin lines from the bottoms of the balloons to the center of the bow.

Caring Card

It's not Valentine's Day without the valentines! Do something different this year, and draw one instead.

Final

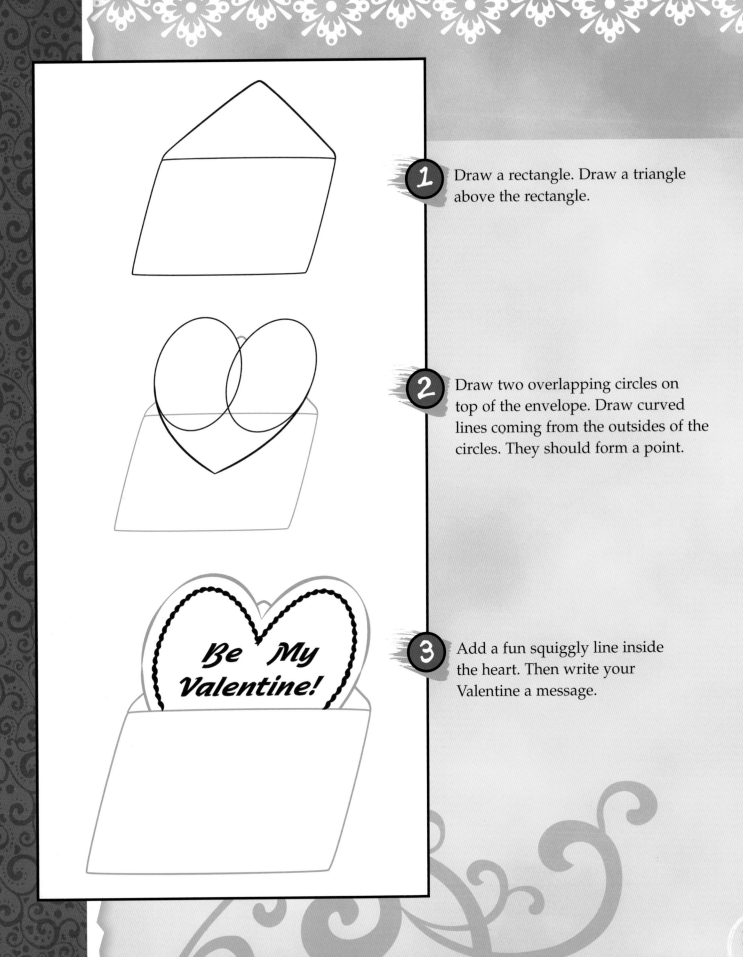

1. Draw a rectangle. Draw a triangle above the rectangle.

2. Draw two overlapping circles on top of the envelope. Draw curved lines coming from the outsides of the circles. They should form a point.

3. Add a fun squiggly line inside the heart. Then write your Valentine a message.

Be My Valentine!

Sweet Treat

A swirl of frosting makes every day better.
Draw these tasty treats. And add your own
sweet message to each one.

HUG ME

BE MINE

TRUE LOVE

Final

1

Start the cupcake by drawing the shape of a chocolate kiss. Use straight lines to add a bottom.

2

Draw curved lines across the cupcake top to start the swirls. Add straight lines on the bottom.

3

Add scalloped lines around the sides of the cupcake top. Draw a heart in the center.

4

Add a detail line to the heart to make it look 3-D.

Roses Are Red

Draw flowers for someone special. Unlike real roses, these beauties will last forever.

Final

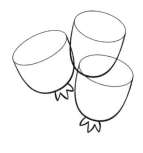

① Draw an oval. Starting on the left side of the oval, draw a half circle up to the right side. Repeat this drawing twice, overlapping them with the first one. On the front two flowers, use jagged lines to draw bottom leaves.

② Add slightly wavy lines along the sides of the flowers. Draw long, thin rectangle stems coming from the flowers with leaves.

③ Draw spiral lines inside each oval. Add a third stem coming from the back flower. Then draw leaves on the stems.

④ Add detail lines to the flowers and leaves.

Holding Hands

Best friends offer helping hands
when you need them most. Celebrate
friendship with this special drawing.

Final

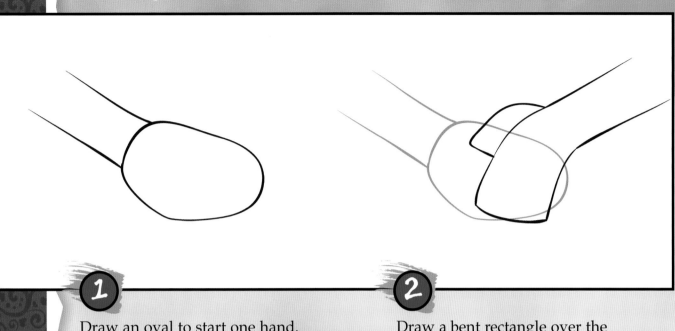

1 Draw an oval to start one hand. Add straight lines coming off the hand as an arm.

2 Draw a bent rectangle over the oval. Add a curved rectangle to start a thumb.

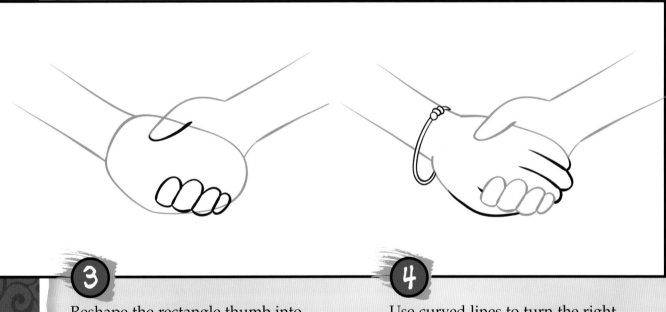

3 Reshape the rectangle thumb into a rounded one. Add small oval fingers to the rectangle hand.

4 Use curved lines to turn the right side of the oval into fingers. Draw two curved lines around the left arm. Add small circle beads to make it a bracelet.

Kitty Cat

Drawing a soft little kitty is the perfect way to show someone you care. It can get anyone out of a bad "mewd."

YOU'RE PURRFECT

Final

1

Draw an oval head. Draw an oval body under the head. Use curved lines to add legs to each side.

2

Use curved and jagged lines to add fur to the face. Draw a "V" shape with a rounded bottom to start the front legs. Add a curvy line to start the tail.

3

Use curved lines to draw ears on the head. Draw two circle eyes. Add a circle in the center of the face. Draw a small circle nose inside it. Draw a half circle on the cat's body. Round out the tail.

4

Draw large ovals around the circle eyes. Add a smile under the nose and a thin line connecting the two. Then draw detail lines on the front of the body to make front legs and feet.

Guppy Love

Let the love bubble up with this drawing. No one will find it fishy at all!

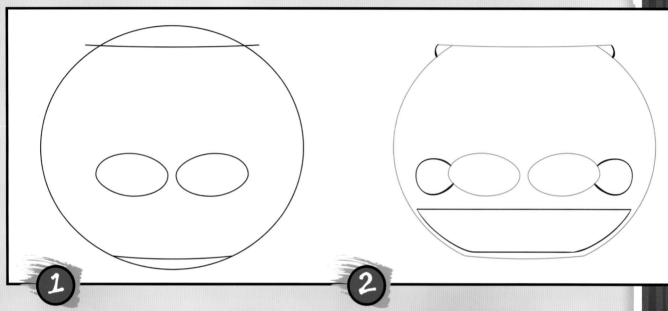

1 Draw a large circle. Add straight lines across the top and bottom. Draw two ovals inside the circle.

2 Add curved lines to the ends of the top line. Draw small circles beside each oval. Add a rounded rectangle to the bottom of the bowl.

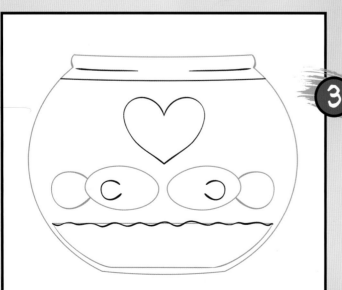

3 Add detail lines to the top of the bowl. Draw a heart in the center. Add a "C" shape to each oval to start fins. Use a scalloped line to make sand at the bottom.

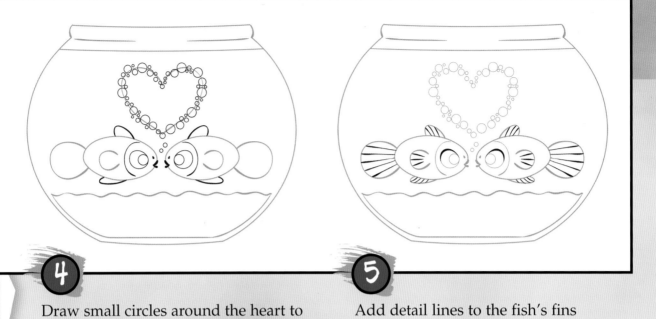

4 Draw small circles around the heart to look like bubbles. Add top and bottom fins to each fish. Also add circle eyes, lips, and detail lines to their faces.

5 Add detail lines to the fish's fins and eyes.

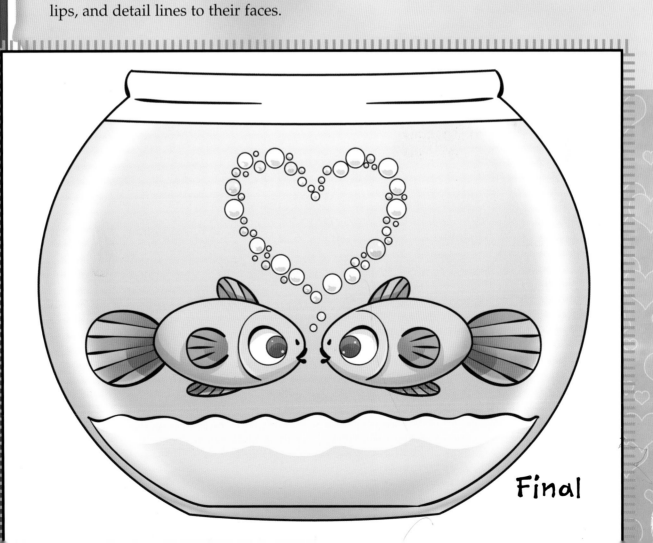

Final

Love Bug

Draw this cute project for someone you love.
When you're done, tuck it under his or her pillow.
This will be one bug nobody minds in bed!

Final

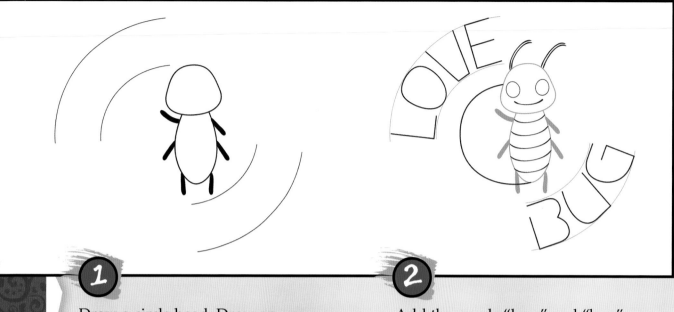

1

Draw a circle head. Draw an oval body below the head. Sketch six rounded legs around the body. Then draw curved lines around the bug.

2

Add the words "love" and "bug" between the curved lines. Draw a half-circle shell on the bug's side. Use curved lines to add stripes, antennae, and a mouth. Draw circle eyes.

3

Make the letters into block letters. Draw circles on the shell. Add small hearts to the ends of the antennae. Draw small circles inside the eyes as pupils.

4

Add fun dot details around the letters.

Baby Bear

He's cute, cuddly, and beary lovable. Draw this little guy to spread joy to everyone you know.

Final

1

Draw an oval head. Add a smaller circle inside the oval. Draw an oval body under the head. Add a smaller oval inside.

2

Draw two half-circle ears on top of the head. Add smaller half circles inside the first. Use scalloped lines to add fur around the head. Draw small oval arms. Then add small circles inside the ovals.

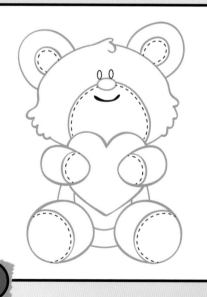

3

Give the bear a circle nose. Draw a heart between its arms. Then draw oval legs. Add small circles inside these ovals too.

4

Draw short lines around the inside circles on the ears, face, arms, and legs. These lines should make the bear look like it was sewn. Then give your bear a smile.

Crazy Cupid

This crazy character only comes out on Valentine's Day. But you can keep Cupid's love around all year with this simple sketch.

1 Draw a circle head. Draw an oval body under the head. Add two rectangle legs. Then use curved lines to draw arms.

2 Draw a curved line inside the head and across the belly. Draw small oval ears. Round out the legs. Draw oval feet. Then give the character oval eyes and a belly button.

3 Use scalloped lines around the head to make curly hair. Draw a long, thin rectangle in one hand. Draw a backward "C" shape in the other. Add detail lines to the sides to make it look like a diaper.

4 Add detail lines to the ears and hands. Draw circles around the eyes. Add a nose. Draw two curved lines to start the mouth. Add a straight line across the "C" shape.

5 Use curvy lines to draw wings. Add a heart and tail to the arrow. Give Cupid some toes. Then add circle cheeks, eyebrows, and eye details. Finally, finish the mouth.

Final

Hugs and Kisses

People give hugs and kisses to celebrate
Valentine's Day. But give this sketch to Mom.
She might just let you skip the smooch.

1

Draw an oval head. Draw another
oval head slightly overlapping the
first. Use straight and curved lines
to start the necks and bodies.

2

Use jagged and curved lines to
start the hair on each head. Add
curved noses and small mouths.
Draw curved and straight lines to
add collars and arms to each body.

3

Use curved and scalloped lines to
add more hair to each head. Give
each character an ear. Add detail
lines to the boy's shirt and arm.

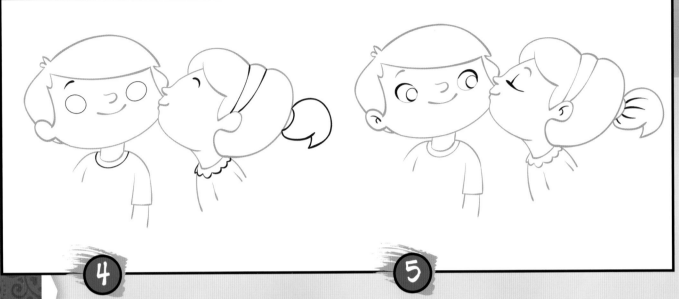

4

Draw circle eyes on the boy. Add eyebrows to each character. Draw detail lines on both shirts. Use curved lines to give the girl a headband and ponytail.

5

On the boy, draw small circles inside the large circles as pupils. Use curved lines to draw an eye on the girl. Add detail lines to her hair and to their ears.

Final

Love Letters

Don't just say "I love you." Draw it! Sketch out these "love" letters. And you'll be sure to have a happy Valentine's Day.

Final

1

Draw two straight lines across the page. On the left end, draw a circle head. Add a rounded body and curved line to start the face.

2

Draw a heart just to the left of the middle. On the right side, draw a circle head. Add a rounded body and a curved line to start the face.

3

Add triangle ears, rounded legs, a tail, and a nose to the dog on the left. Then add detail lines to its neck and feet. Draw an "L" between the straight lines over the dog. Draw two smaller hearts inside the first one.

4

Draw a "V" and an "E" to the right of the heart. Add a triangle ear, rounded legs, a tail, a nose, and a mouth to the dog on the right. Add detail lines to its neck and feet.

continued on next page

5

Add detail lines to the letters. Draw small circles inside the heart. Use curvy lines to add fur to both dogs' heads. Add detail lines to their bodies.

6

Close up the letters to make them block letters. Add detail lines to the heart. Draw big circle eyes on each dog. Finish by giving them each eyebrows and adding detail lines to their mouths and noses.

Your Sketches

Your Sketches

Your Sketches

YOU'RE PURRFECT

Your Sketches

Your Sketches